OVERVIEW

Overview

Employees spend a large part of their lives at work. Their relationships with their peers help determine how productive and enjoyable this time is. In the workplace, peers can provide friendship, support, mentoring, and help on the job.

Having good relationships with peers boosts employees' confidence levels. Employees are more able to find support for their ambitions, and are better able to solve problems with the help of others.

All this makes for happier and more productive employees.

Good peer relationships also have many benefits for an organization. For example, friends at work are more likely to share information and help each other out. This leads to higher productivity and better problem solving. Also, when employees have good relationships, they feel more positive about going to work and are typically more loyal to the organization. This results in higher attendance and lower attrition, or turnover.

Sorin Dumitrascu

In this book, you'll learn what a peer relationship is, how it differs from other types of relationships you may have, and what general expectations govern professional relationships. You'll learn about the benefits of good peer relationships for organizations. Finally, you'll learn how to cultivate peer relationships that contribute to your own and your organization's success.

There's no such thing as a workplace without office politics. It's natural that, in any organization, individuals and departments try to achieve their work goals partly through their professional relationships with others. It's also natural that, in any group of people, some exert more influence than others and are more successful in obtaining the support they need.

Participating in office politics doesn't have to be petty, malicious, or coldly manipulative. Instead, it can involve recognizing that part of what contributes to anyone's success in the work environment is how well an individual – or a group – gets along with and influences others.

Using office politics to your advantage involves focusing on building mutually beneficial professional relationships that will further your goals and the goals of your organization.

It's important not to confuse personal relationships with those that are professional. Because you spend lot of time at work, it's likely that you've developed personal relationships and that you work with good friends. However, it's the successful professional relationships – those you have with people in a work capacity – that can help you achieve your work-related goals.

Peer Relationships

In this book, you'll learn to be more aware of the political relationships in your workplace and of your colleagues' personal approaches to politics.

You'll learn how to identify the key peers who can significantly affect your ability to do your work well and to achieve your goals. Finally, you'll learn how to build and maintain strategic professional relationships with your key peers.

CHAPTER 1 - The Value of Peer Relationships

CHAPTER 1 - The Value of Peer Relationships

Section 1 - Peer Relationships at Work

Section 2 - Organizational Benefits of Peer Relationships

Section 3 - Cultivating Peer Relationships for Personal Goals

Section 1 - Peer Relationships at Work

Section 1 - Peer Relationships at Work

Cultivating good peer relationships at work improves both job satisfaction and performance. A peer relationship is one between equals, and may be personal or professional. Being able to separate personal and professional aspects of your relationships with others is very important.

Personal and professional relationships have different purposes, are characterized by different communication styles, and are based on different rules and assumptions.

In professional relationships, you're expected to act professionally at all times, show respect to your colleagues, communicate often and clearly, serve as a trusted confidante to others, and encourage honest, but tactful, feedback.

Peer relationships

Peer relationships

People connect with one another in a variety of ways. These connections, or relationships, impact how people feel, think, and behave. This applies in the workplace as much as it does in any other environment. Sometimes in subtle ways and sometimes more directly, our relationships with people at work affect our job satisfaction and work performance.

The way you interact with your supervisors at work or with people you manage is very important. What's sometimes overlooked, however, is the importance of the relationships between employees who occupy a similar position in an organization's hierarchy. These relationships are among the most significant. When considering these relationships, it's useful to distinguish between the terms "colleague" and "peer."

Colleague

Peer Relationships

A colleague is any coworker or employee in your company who has no enforceable authority over you and who you don't supervise.

A colleague may be a teammate, an employee from another department, or any other person at work who has no explicit authority over you. You may be friends with a colleague, you may be casual acquaintances, or you may never even have met.

Peer

A peer is someone who works at the same level as you in an organization. A peer is also a coworker, but, unlike other types of coworkers, is important to your work.

Neither person in a peer relationship has formal authority over the other. The definition of a peer is relative though and depends on context. For example, you can have a peer relationship with a direct report outside of work – although at work, you're no longer peers.

Good relationships among peers and colleagues lead to better teamwork and collaboration within and between departments. They also provide employees with the support and encouragement they need, resulting in better overall morale and higher productivity.

Inter-functional relationships can be between colleagues or peers. These relationships are between employees from different departments.

When inter-functional relationships work well, they let everyone involved leverage a variety of skills and expertise. For example, copy writers and designers might collaborate effectively on an advertising campaign. Alternatively, employees in an organization's Finance Department might work closely with Human Resources personnel when determining how best to restructure an organization's workforce to achieve required cost cuts.

When you develop these relationships, keep in mind that office politics can play a significant role. Feelings of ownership and territoriality within departments can be problems if not handled carefully.

Although good peer relationships are supportive, organizations don't assemble people with the intention of forming support groups. For an organization, the primary purpose of work relationships is to accomplish tasks and organizational goals.

Any peer relationship can be complicated because it involves two simultaneous types of relationships – personal and professional. For example, you may be friends outside of work with your manager. In this personal relationship, you're peers – your manager has no formal authority over your personal life and you interact as equals. At work, however, you and your manager are not peers because your manager has formal authority over you.

The types of bonds you form with your peers depend on your social skills and the receptivity of others toward you. Knowing how best to create positive bonds with your peers can change your work experience for the better.

Question

What are the characteristics of peer work relationships?

Options:

1. They can be both personal and professional

2. Their definition is relative and based on levels of authority in the workplace

3. They occur between coworkers who have the same levels of authority

Peer Relationships

4. They occur between people who affect, or are important to, one another's work

5. They can occur between managers and subordinates

6. They occur only between people working in different departments

Answer

Option 1: This option is correct. Peers may have work relationships but also be friends and socialize with one another.

Option 2: This is a correct option. Neither person in a peer relationship has formal authority over the other. Also, you may have a personal peer relationship with someone outside of work, but be under that person's authority at work, so you wouldn't be peers in the workplace.

Option 3: This option is correct. Neither person in a peer relationship has formal authority over the other. So managers and their subordinates, for example, don't have peer relationships in the workplace although they may work together.

Option 4: This option is correct. Peers are important to your work even though they don't have formal authority over you.

Option 5: This option is incorrect. Neither person in a peer relationship has formal authority over the other. However, it's true that a manager and a subordinate may have a peer relationship outside work.

Option 6: This is an incorrect option. Peer relationships can, but don't necessarily, occur between employees in different departments.

Personal versus professional relationships

To manage peer relationships successfully in the workplace, you need to be able to distinguish between your personal and professional relationships. These types of relationships differ in terms of their purpose and their emotional importance to people. They also involve different communication styles, rules, and assumptions.

Purpose

The purpose of personal relationships is to build rapport and provide mutual support, whereas the purpose of professional relationships is to accomplish job-related tasks.

For example, you might strengthen a personal relationship by having lunch with a colleague and chatting about family life and interests. As part of a professional relationship, you might have a business lunch with a colleague to coordinate efforts to release a new product successfully.

In practice, you may relate in both personal and professional ways with a peer during a single lunch meeting – but it's still important to recognize how your purpose differs in each case.

Emotional importance

Personal relationships can be very important to people, and the loss of a personal friend can be emotionally painful. The loss of a professional relationship may cause difficulties at work, but doesn't usually cause emotional discomfort.

For example, if a close friend from work relocates to another city, you might miss this person. However, if a team member who you hardly ever spoke to leaves, you might find it difficult to complete your work, but you probably wouldn't feel an emotional loss.

Methods of communication

Communication is generally more formal for professional relationships than for personal ones. Also, it's generally acceptable to tell people you relate to professionally what to do or what you require – whereas in personal relationships, you'd ask, rather than expect, a requirement to be met.

For example, a peer at work might say "Please submit the report to me by 4:00 p.m." and this wouldn't be offensive. In a personal relationship, you'd ask if a friend could meet you at 4:00 p.m. rather than telling this person to do so.

Rules

Far fewer rules govern personal relationships compared to professional ones. For instance, you can choose to end a personal relationship at any time. And it's mostly just the people involved in the relationship who define the types of behavior that are considered acceptable. You can generally act silly around a friend and even shout at her, whereas this wouldn't be considered acceptable in a professional context.

In professional relationships, you need to act professionally at all times. This involves adhering to various unwritten rules, or norms, as well as to more explicit company rules governing behavior. It's also not acceptable to leave a task undone or to refuse a work-related task because you don't want to work with a peer.

Assumptions

In personal relationships, the assumption exists that everyone is equal and has a choice. Neither person has power over the other and you can choose whether to associate with one another. Either person is free to refuse a relationship initially or to end a relationship.

In professional relationships, you need to work together whether you like one another personally or not.

Suppose Janice and Jason work at a shipping company. They have been friends and colleagues for several years. Recently Jason was promoted and now plays the role of Janice's supervisor.

In their professional relationship, Jason is expected to assign tasks to Janice and report on her competence in carrying out the tasks.

In their personal relationship, Jason has no authority over Janice. Should their working and personal relationships overlap, or should Jason adopt the role of Janice's superior outside of the workplace, tension might arise between them. Any such confusion of relationships should be addressed directly.

Question

How do personal relationships differ from professional relationships in the workplace?

Options:

1. Their purpose is to provide support
2. They involve greater emotional involvement
3. They're based on the assumption that people can end the relationships at any point
4. They're characterized by formal methods of communication
5. They're subject to more clearly defined rules

Answer

Option 1: This option is correct. The purpose of personal relationships is to build rapport and provide mutual support. Professional relationships, however, are established to accomplish organizational tasks.

Option 2: This is a correct option. People invest more emotionally in personal relationships than in professional ones.

Option 3: This option is correct. Personal relationships are based on the assumptions of equality and choice – either party can choose whether to continue the relationship. This freedom doesn't typically exist in professional relationships.

Option 4: This option is incorrect. Professional relationships are characterized by more formal methods of communication. It's in personal relationships that people tend to communicate informally.

Option 5: This is an incorrect option. In personal relationships, few rules are clearly defined and the people involved mostly determine the types of behavior that are acceptable. Those involved can also choose to end the relationship at any point. In professional relationships, a variety of rules – both unwritten and explicit – govern behavior at all times.

Professional expectations

Professional expectations

A range of expectations and norms governs all professional interactions between people. They help ensure a harmonious working environment. These expectations and norms hold true whether or not you also have personal relationships with the people involved.

Follow along as Janice interacts with Jason at work.

Jason: Hi Janice. Do you have the report ready yet?

Janice: No. The whole thing is just ridiculous and I don't want to do it. I think the whole reasoning behind this change is just stupid.

Janice reacts angrily.

Jason: Janice, the deadline is today. Getting the report in is part of your job. Your personal feelings about this just don't factor in.

Jason responds angrily.

Janice: I don't care. I wasn't consulted about this change, and you know it's my area of expertise. I have enough work to do without having to waste my time on this.

Although this conversation may be appropriate in Janice and Jason's personal relationship, it's not acceptable in their professional relationship. Janice has failed to comply with certain key expectations of professional relationships.

Key expectations of a professional relationship include acting professionally at all times, showing respect for colleagues, communicating well, serving as a trusted confidante, and encouraging feedback.

Acting professionally

In your professional relationships, you're expected to act professionally at all times. This includes dressing appropriately, using suitably formal language, and behaving in a measured fashion.

You should avoid behavior, including the use of bad language that could be offensive to others. You should act politely in all situations.

Respect

In professional relationships, you're expected to treat your coworkers with respect. This includes respecting their right to an opinion, and respecting their time and space.

So you should remain polite, fulfill agreements or give notice if you're unable to do so in time, and assume that everyone you work with has the same goal of completing their work successfully.

Communicating well

If you communicate with those you work with often and openly, it ensures everyone can solve problems more easily. It also helps build your professional relationships.

When you communicate, attempt to find out how you can be helpful and build alliances with those in your own department and across departments.

Serving as a confidante

As a professional, you're expected to listen to others and to treat information you're given as confidential. So you should avoid gossiping or passing on information that's meant to be kept private.

Encouraging feedback

In professional relationships, you're expected to encourage honest, but tactful, feedback. This involves discussing how you and others are performing. Provided it's delivered in a respectful way and is accurate, honest feedback can help you and others grow.

Follow along as Jason and his coworker Nikki demonstrate some of the behaviors expected in a professional relationship.

Nikki: Hi Jason. I need your opinion on how to handle a difficult customer. Do you have a minute to discuss it with me?

Jason: Actually, I've got my hands full at the moment. Could we discuss it a little later – say at 2:00 p.m. this afternoon?

Nikki: Thanks for the offer Jason, but I need to speak to the customer before lunch. Is there something I can do to help you get through your work so that we have some time?

Jason: I'm so sorry, but it's all stuff I have to do myself. You are pretty good at being diplomatic, but if you're worried about logistical issues, you could talk to Janice, who really excels in that area. I think she could really help build your confidence in that regard.

Nikki: Thanks Jason. It is a logistical issue. I'll go and speak to Janice.

Jason and Nikki have a strong professional relationship, meeting four of the five expectations in one conversation. Despite having important issues or tasks to deal with, they remain professional and polite. Nikki shows respect for Jason's time by asking him if he has a moment to discuss a problem. Both are open and honest with each other, and try to assist one another. Finally, Jason provides Nikki with feedback about her strengths and weaknesses, and provides a potential solution.

When you listen attentively to those you work with, you open the door to stronger professional relationships. If others feel confident that you'll listen respectfully, they're more likely to tell you about work difficulties and opportunities, allowing for better problem solving.

So being a confidante to coworkers strengthens professional relationships, builds alliances, and helps you to be happier and more successful in your job.

Question

Which statements reflect the expectations that govern professional relationships?

Options:

1. "I always try to be polite to colleagues and informed about what is happening at work."

2. "I listen very carefully to what my coworkers have to say and don't gossip."

3. "I only ever shout at colleagues when they act very unprofessionally."

4. "I speak to my colleagues regularly about what is going on and what work issues need to be resolved."

5. "I never point out where a colleague has made a mistake."

Answer

Option 1: This option is correct. The statement shows a commitment to acting professionally at all times. Other factors involved in acting professionally include using suitably formal language, behaving in a measured, mature fashion, and dressing appropriately.

Option 2: This is a correct option. You need to listen well and respect confidences if you're to become a trusted confidante. This is one of the expectations of a professional relationship.

Option 3: This option is incorrect. Shouting at a colleague or any other person at work is an example of failing to behave professionally, irrespective of what provokes the behavior. In a professional context, it's expected that you'll remain respectful to colleagues at all times.

Option 4: This option is correct. It's expected that, as a professional, you'll communicate clearly and often with those you work with. This makes it easier for everyone to solve problems and helps prevent misunderstandings that could lead to work errors or conflict.

Option 5: This is an incorrect option. It's expected that, as a professional, you'll encourage honest feedback. This includes receiving and giving constructive criticism in a positive and supportive way.

Section 2 - Organizational Benefits of Peer Relationships

Strong and positive peer relationships provide a range of benefits for an organization. These include high rates of attendance and longevity of service, more partnerships and collaboration, and better workflow. They also include better harnessing of employees' unique abilities, and greater likelihood of achieving collective organizational goals.

The more individuals at work care about one another, the stronger their team player attitude. This attitude means that employees focus more on advancing group goals than personal goals, and take care of one another as a way of advancing these goals. So strong interpersonal relationships help support an organization's collective efforts.

Benefits of good peer relationships

Healthy interpersonal relationships among peers at work mean a more productive and harmonious organization as a whole. If everyone works well together, an organization can benefit financially through reduced turnover and increased productivity. Organizations that maintain constructive peer relationships also benefit culturally, with happier employees who work together well.

Good peer relationships also have a number of other benefits for organizations. At an individual level, these include high rates of employee attendance and longevity of service, and better harnessing of employees' unique abilities.

Attendance and longevity

A Gallup survey found that having a best friend at work was a key indicator of work satisfaction. So to feel good about your job, it helps to have good relationships with your peers.

When employees are happier at work, they tend to perform better and identify more with the organization. They are less likely to take sick leave or to move to another organization.

Having good relationships at work helps you to look forward to the time you spend there and to feel as though you belong with the organization.

Harnessing of abilities

If you have good relationships with your peers, you can help one another to identify and harness your unique abilities. This bolsters individual growth, which in turn benefits the whole organization.

For instance, if you find out that a colleague works as a trainer and facilitator at a local charity, you can motivate her to use her skills at work to assist in training coworkers. Additionally, having your own skills and talents noticed and appreciated can serve as a great motivator in your work.

Good peer relationships also have benefits for organizations because they encourage people to work together more effectively. When employees from different stages of a production line communicate well, processes tend to run more smoothly, so there's better workflow. Also, employees who have good relationships with one another are more likely to give and receive favors to resolve holdups and glitches. Stronger partnerships and better collaboration across functions result in better efficiency.

Say a project manager notices a discrepancy in a set of figures just before she is due to deliver them to the

Peer Relationships

program manager. If she has a good relationship with the program manager, it's likely she'll let him know about the possible delay. He may be able to offer suggestions that could resolve the discrepancies or negotiate a new deadline with the project manager. This is just one example of how good peer relationships can help facilitate a better, smoother workflow.

If you get along well with peers, you're also more likely to help them – or be offered their help – in overcoming the everyday glitches that otherwise cause bottlenecks or delays. For example, if you're friends with the person you inform about the problem you're having with a set of figures, this person is more likely to offer help or to suggest someone else who can.

Similarly, if your computer malfunctions and you have a good relationship with someone in your IT Department, that person is likely to help you out quicker.

Relationships across the workflow help keep employees informed about what's happening outside their immediate spheres of influence. This provides a more holistic view of the organization and means that employee contributions can be more strategic.

In most organizations, the work done by different employees is interconnected. So to meet targets, organizations require strong partnerships and collaboration.

Failure to meet deadlines has a run-on effect that can be devastating, so team members must be aware of how delays in their work affect their colleagues.

Strong partnerships ensure communication flow and motivate people to perform to ensure their entire team is successful. When employees share credit for accomplishments and acknowledge collaboration, individuals feel appreciated and work better together.

All together, these individual and team benefits add up to a final benefit of good peer relationships – they make it more likely that an organization will achieve its collective goals and objectives. Whether in service or manufacturing environments, motivated employees who reliably attend work, collaborate with one another. They have a better chance of meeting organizational goals than employees who are isolated and unhappy.

Kyra

"Our corporate goal is to build the company's customer base and reduce the number of service complaints. I find that the regular updates from technical support about known software problems really helps me deal with clients more professionally. I don't have to search for answers while I have a client on the line. Instead, I am able to handle most of the queries myself or I can transfer the client to a colleague I know will have the answer. Also, knowing people well at work really helps reduce the stress of my job. I actually look forward to work and meeting my friends."

Mario

"Our motto is high-quality paints and on-time delivery. I believe I help the company get closer to this goal. I noticed that Paulo was a really meticulous person and that he had a knack for finding shortcuts that didn't reduce the quality of our work. We discussed this in our weekly team meeting and Paulo was selected for training as a supervisor in quality control. And you know, since he's been working there, all our jobs have become simpler. We

Peer Relationships

make fewer mistakes, because he knows what it's like doing this job and encourages us all to share what works."

Question

Which statements describe the organizational benefits of peer relationships?

Options:

1. "I like getting up for work in the morning, because I know I'll be spending time with good people. I've been working for the same company for several years now."

2. "Because a friend at work noticed my animation skills, I now design animations for our web site."

3. "I'm not sure when I'll receive work from our writers, so I use the time to gather background information on world news."

4. "Our sales team worked so well together that we not only met our target, we exceeded it."

5. "We work pretty much in isolation and, because there are fewer distractions, I get a lot done."

Answer

Option 1: This option is correct. The statement highlights the good attendance and longevity of service that positive peer relationships can bring.

Option 2: This is a correct option. This statement highlights how peers help each other harness their unique abilities, providing better quality and a range of talent for the organization.

Option 3: This is an incorrect option. Better peer relationships in this situation would provide better workflow.

Option 4: This option is correct. This statement highlights how the organization is more likely to meet their collective goals and objectives when peer relationships are good.

Option 5: This option is incorrect. Good peer relationships should generate more organizational partnerships and encourage collaboration.

Team players

Team players

When people in an organization work effectively as a team, almost anything seems possible. Strong interpersonal relationships help support an organization's collective efforts and encourage a "team player" attitude among employees.

Strong peer relationships mean that individual members care about the success of others. This fosters the team player attitude of wanting to advance group goals.

For example, team players are more likely to help a team member who is behind or battling with work so that a project can be completed successfully. So team players look after others as a way of advancing group goals.

Team players are likely to play by the rules but will use office politics where appropriate to advance collective, rather than individual, goals. For example, if the team needs better technology to achieve its goals, a team player is likely to trade favors to leverage connections within the IT Department and at management level to try to get this technology for the team.

Team players have to be careful not to be taken advantage of when helping achieve collective goals or the goals of others.

For example, they may take on low-prestige chores and not work on areas that they want to advance in. So team players also need to find an individual voice and to balance personal and group goals.

Strong interpersonal relationships help support an organization's collective efforts. This attitude is characteristic of team players, who prioritize collective goals over individual ones. Positive peer relationships encourage the kinds of behaviors associated with team players.

Question

Which are attributes of team players?

Options:

1. They help advance the goals of the group
2. They play by the rules, but will use office politics where appropriate to advance a collective objective
3. They look after others as a way of advancing group goals
4. They have to be careful not to be taken advantage of when helping achieve collective goals or goals of others at their own expense
5. They operate best in highly political environments
6. They are often less productive than highly individual employees

Answer

Option 1: This option is correct. Team players try to advance collective goals, or the goals of the group, rather than their own individual agenda.

Option 2: This is a correct option. Team players generally play by the rules, but may exchange favors or use their leverage to advance a collective objective. So they aren't opposed to using office politics, but use this for group, rather than individual, advancement.

Option 3: This option is correct. Team players believe that you get ahead through helping and taking care of others. They try to ensure that the team is strong to ensure success.

Option 4: This is a correct option. Because team players prioritize the goals of the team or group, they may help others at their own expense. So they need to find a balance between their individual ambitions and the success of the group.

Option 5: This option is incorrect. Actually, team players thrive in a moderately political environment rather than a highly political one. They will use office politics for advancing the interests of a group rather than their own personal interests.

Option 6: This option is incorrect. Team players are often highly productive and, through collaborative effort, boost productivity across the board.

Jason, who was recently promoted to a supervisory position at his shipping company, enjoys working with his team members. He often helps out less-experienced employees, providing his time or skills and pointing them to other employees who can provide the information or assistance they need.

He often provides favors for the IT Department and for Marketing, and tries to ensure that people in these departments prioritize his team's needs. He had wanted to make a shift into human resource management and development, but decided against it because the company had too few people with his particular skill set.

Question

Do you think Jason has all of the attributes required of a team player?

Options:

1. Yes
2. No

Answer

Option 1: This is the correct option. Jason prioritizes collective goals over individual ones and tries to look after others as a means to advance group goals. He is also willing to use office politics to help the team. This attitude is characteristic of team players.

Option 2: This option is incorrect. Team players work to advance the goals of the group through helping others and through appropriate use of office politics. Team players prioritize collective goals over individual goals. Jason's approach demonstrates all of these team player characteristics.

Section 3 - Cultivating Peer Relationships for Personal Goals

Section 3 - Cultivating Peer Relationships for Personal Goals

Developing strong peer relationships at work can enhance your career and can make your work easier and more enjoyable. To cultivate these relationships, you should try always to do what you say you're going to do, help others, avoid gossip, share your enjoyment of work, and treat your peers with respect.

Individual benefits

As an employee, you can benefit in several ways from having positive relationships with your peers at work. Effective work relationships form the foundation for promotions, pay raises, goal accomplishments, and job satisfaction.

Developing strong peer relationships can have several personal benefits:
- they can help you achieve your personal goals,
- they can improve your job performance,
- they can improve your professional reputation,
- they can encourage the exchange of favors, and
- they can gain you significant learning opportunities.

Achieve personal goals

Having the support, or at least the respect, of your peers at work helps you to achieve your goals and build self-confidence. Colleagues can access their own networks on your behalf. This can put you in touch with others who have the skills or influence you need to move in the direction you want to go.

Improve performance

When you feel the support of your colleagues and they share information and skills, your self- confidence and your technical abilities improve. In turn, this improves your performance and efficiency on the job.

Improve your reputation

You gain credibility and a good reputation from being helpful, sharing your knowledge, and paying attention to others so you can respond with small acts of kindness or thoughtfulness.

To show your integrity, you need to be clear about your area of expertise and knowledge, strive to learn more in these areas, and communicate what you can do. You should also acknowledge your mistakes when necessary.

Exchange favors

The foundation in building relationships is reciprocity. If you find ways to help others, they are more inclined to help you. Then as you mutually help each other, your relationship grows in strength.

Always consider what you have to offer and how you can add value – ineffective help isn't really help at all. For example, you can help colleagues when they're struggling, mentor those with less experience, and find processes or issues that you can offer to fix.

Gain learning opportunities

You can learn a great deal from your peers when working collaboratively with them. They can teach you about organizational culture and politics, as well as basic skills and knowledge, so that you can achieve more in your work. If you visit peers and speak and work with them, learning opportunities are likely to open up.

Peers can also coach one another, solving real issues, recommending readings or training courses, and providing visual, audio, and experiential training. You also learn through modeling behavior, identifying your needs, and asking for honest feedback from your peers.

Generally, you learn best when you mix the learning environments and the learning styles to which you're exposed.

When you aim to achieve your personal goals at work, you need to identify key figures that could help you grow. It's often helpful to find a mentor and to connect with your mentor's network of contacts so that you can learn and grow.

When Nikki first began working at the shipping company, Jason was assigned as her mentor. Through Jason's advice, Nikki's skills improved – and through his contacts, she was able to build alliances that positioned her well for promotion.

Nikki made alliances across company functions. So when things went wrong, Nikki could offer to help or could call on favors from others. As a result, Nikki gained a reputation for efficiency and helpfulness – qualities that make her stand out against other candidates for promotion.

Follow along as Nikki and Sharon, another of Nikki's peers, build their relationship and benefit from doing this.

Nikki: Thanks for that spreadsheet tip, it's really made generating reports so much easier.

Sharon: It's my pleasure. I'm glad you're finding it useful. In truth, accounting is my real skill, but I'm trying to develop my presentation and training skills. I'd like to move into that area more.

Nikki: Maybe I could help. I used to develop and coordinate training at my old job. I delivered presentations every month.

Sharon: Really? I never knew that. That would be great Nikki. I really appreciate your offer.

In the conversation between Nikki and Sharon, the spreadsheet tip helped Nikki become more efficient at work. Sharon strengthens her credibility by being clear about her area of expertise and, in an exchange of favors, Nikki offers to coach Sharon so that she can move closer to her goal, which is to develop her presentation and training skills. Both learn from each other and mutually benefit each other.

Question

What are the benefits you can gain from building positive peer relationships?

Options:

1. They help you to achieve your personal goals at work
2. They help you to work more efficiently
3. They encourage the exchange of favors
4. They enable you to build credibility and improve your reputation
5. They help you to learn more about your job and the organization
6. They help you become better qualified in your chosen field
7. They help you focus on the tasks at hand

Answer

Option 1: This option is correct. Through the alliances you make and through what you learn in your interactions with peers, you become better positioned to achieve your goals at work.

Option 2: This is a correct option. Learning from others' experience and using a network of favors across departments helps you to work more efficiently.

Option 3: This option is correct. Making positive connections enables you to notice when someone needs help or support. When you do favors, coworkers are more willing to do the same for you. The result is positive collaboration.

Option 4: This option is correct. By being helpful and showing integrity in what you do and say, you build your credibility and reputation. This may place you in line for pay raises, promotions, or move you closer to your personal goals at work.

Option 5: This is a correct option. Strong peer relationships provide learning opportunities where you gain knowledge and skills and you gain greater access to information. Interfunctional relationships help you to get a broader view of the organization.

Option 6: This is an incorrect option. Although you can gain knowledge and skills from your peers, you need formal education to improve your qualifications.

Option 7: This option is incorrect. Although strong peer relationships can boost your efficiency through learning skills and tips, your level of focus is an internal attribute that isn't directly tied to your relationships with others.

Being reliable

Being reliable

Follow along as Luke and Carrie talk about a new marketing campaign at work, noting how they build their relationship.

Luke: Did you get the brief about our new marketing campaign? It sounds really exciting.

Carrie: Yes. I love the color palette. I've been trying to come up with the right fonts to use.

Luke: Well, I know the images that we have lined up have quite sharp and clear lines, nothing really rounded. Does that help?

Carrie: Yes. That's really useful thanks. Would you mind giving me some feedback on the layout I used for the in-house magazine last month? I wasn't very confident that it worked and want to know what I could have done differently.

Luke: Well, I really liked how you integrated images with text – it gave the layout an edge. Sometimes though, the spreads were a bit busy. Perhaps you could use a more uniform color palette and slightly less text. Something that's similar to what you did in the brochures we released last week.

In their conversation, Luke and Carrie demonstrated a number of the strategies you can use to cultivate strong peer relationships. Six strategies are particularly helpful – always do what you say you're going to do, be helpful, don't gossip, enjoy your work and share your enthusiasm for it, treat others with respect, and provide positive feedback.

The first three strategies broadly relate to being reliable at work. If you can be relied on to do what you say, be helpful, and not to gossip, you'll find your colleagues are more likely to respect you and to be helpful in return.

Do what you say

When you always do what you say, you develop a reputation for being dependable and trustworthy. This provides a solid basis for peer relationships.

Doing what you say means you are on time for meetings, complete work to deadline, and share important work-related information with others. For example, if you can't make a deadline, you can provide an early warning of this to those who are waiting for you to complete your work.

You also need to make sure you don't overcommit yourself because you may disappoint people when you can't keep your promises.

Be helpful

Peer Relationships

Being helpful to colleagues and peers requires you to pay attention to them, so you can notice when they need help and respond proactively. Even when you're busy, taking a few minutes to act kindly to someone is worthwhile. It will make your and your colleagues' day just that much better.

For instance, you can help move files into the boardroom, share a useful article, or proofread a colleague's presentation. You could also inform a new recruit of when it's best to take queries to a supervisor. Each act of kindness helps to build better working relationships.

Don't gossip

Gossiping involves talking about others, particularly others' private lives, when there may or may not be any grounding in fact. Gossiping at work has several very negative outcomes, one of which is that it prevents you from forming positive peer relationships.

People may attribute the negative traits to you instead of the person you are gossiping about. Secondly, if your colleagues regard you as a chronic gossip, they are likely to avoid you or avoid sharing with you. It also is very unprofessional and is likely to tarnish your reputation as a trustworthy and credible colleague.

Think about a time when you had to wait for someone to arrive at a scheduled meeting or when a person failed to arrive at all.

If people fail to do what they've said they would, they get a reputation for being unreliable – and others may feel disrespected.

When you do what you say you're going to do, you build credibility with others and show respect toward them. If you make a mistake or forget something, apologize and take steps to ensure it doesn't happen again.

Remember some of the characteristics of a good peer relationship are to act professionally, treat colleagues with respect, and communicate clearly and often. If you model this behavior, it amounts to doing what you say you'll do.

When managing gossip, it's best to avoid discussions that may seem critical of others or your organization. Strategies that may help are to avoid discussions about personal or financial issues and discuss business and current events instead, state your loyalty to your organization, ask to include the person being discussed, or leave the conversation when it turns to gossip. Remember that strong peer relationships require that you behave as a trusted confidante.

Question

What are examples of ways you can cultivate peer relationships to help you achieve your personal goals?

Options:

1. Arrive for meetings on time and switch off your cell phone

2. Offer to research design methods to help your team find more efficient ways to process images

3. Excuse yourself from a conversation that is about the private life of a colleague

4. Commiserate with a colleague when she is talking about how disorganized management is

5. Offer to source images for the company newsletter, although you've never done something like this before

Answer

Option 1: This option is correct. By showing up on time and paying attention, you do what you say you're going to do. This builds your reputation as dependable and trustworthy, and shows respect to your peers.

Option 2: This is a correct option. Helping others involves noticing where you can use your skills or knowledge, or simply where you can provide an act of kindness. It's important that when you help others, you can deliver on what you promise.

Option 3: This option is correct. You can cultivate peer relationships by avoiding gossip. This builds your reputation as a confidante and prevents people from avoiding conversations with you for fear of your potential indiscretion.

Option 4: This option is incorrect. Complaining about the organization or others is a form of gossip and should be avoided if you hope to build strong relationships.

Option 5: This is an incorrect option. It's important not to offer help unless you're qualified to provide it. If you fail to deliver on what you've offered, you'll gain a reputation for being unreliable or untrustworthy.

Being positive

Being positive

The final three strategies for cultivating peer relationships involve being positive in your approach to your work and others. When you enjoy your work, it seems easier to do and others are drawn to your enthusiasm. You must treat your colleagues with respect if you want to form positive relationships. It's also a key characteristic of a professional relationship. The final strategy is to provide positive feedback to peers, acknowledging their successes and helping them grow.

Benefits of enjoying your work

When you enjoy your work, you're more likely to enjoy the company of your colleagues and have positive feelings about your company. People are drawn to others who are positive about work because this attitude is infectious. When you frequently complain, colleagues are likely to start avoiding you.

So enjoying your work, and sharing your positive feelings about the work with those around you, provides greater opportunities for building positive peer relationships.

You also affect those around you by the way you treat them. There are specific behaviors you can use to show respect to others – you should be polite, listen to others, be inclusive, and be open to change.

Be polite

You behave respectfully if you are polite and treat others with kindness. Insulting or constantly criticizing others or their ideas is disrespectful and can be considered a form of bullying.

You need to praise people more than you criticize them. And, if you take the time to notice what others do well, this task should be easy.

Listen to others

To respect colleagues, you need to listen to them and what they have to say before you respond to them. This behavior encourages colleagues to express their ideas and opinions, which provides opportunities for connection and learning.

Be inclusive

Being inclusive involves treating others fairly and equally, no matter what their age, race, gender, or other characteristics. So you should give others the opportunity to share their opinions or knowledge if something that you do will affect them.

Be open to change

When you listen to others' ideas and use those to change or improve your work, you show respect for their ideas and opinions. Being open to change requires an openness to the differences in others and the value that these differences can bring.

Before providing feedback, you need to confirm whether the person actually wants your feedback. So if you haven't been specifically invited to comment, ask if the person would appreciate feedback first. If the feedback includes constructive criticism, it's best to use the format known as a "feedback sandwich." Start by pointing out what the person does right, what didn't work as well, and then point out what strengths the person has that can help solve the issue.

When you provide feedback in the form of the "feedback sandwich," you need to be careful to provide a good balance between what your peers did well and how they could improve. This balance is best achieved when you focus on solutions for improvement.

However, remember that the best approach to delivering feedback depends partly on to whom you're giving the feedback and on your relationship to this person. Sometimes it's best to offer to explore solutions with your peers rather than attempting to spell out what you think they should do to improve.

Another way to ensure balanced and constructive feedback is to ensure you first consider what a person has done in context. If someone has broken a rule for a good reason, for instance, you don't need to point out the violation.

Always ensure your motive for giving feedback is to support and help your peer, rather than to show off what you know.

Finally, if you speak honestly and kindly about how a peer's behavior affects you, this person is more likely to seriously consider your feedback.

Follow along as Nikki provides positive feedback to Sharon after Sharon's presentation.

Nikki: Sharon, you did a great job with the presentation on our company's income statement. I really learned a lot about how to approach problems more creatively.

Sharon: Thanks Nikki. I was a bit worried about trying to fit in too much information in such a short time.

Nikki: I'm sure! You really managed to cover a lot of information. I did get a bit confused at the beginning though. I find that if you provide an overview or set of objectives at the start of a presentation, your audience is more prepared for what's to follow.

Sharon: That's a good point. I'll try it next time.

Nikki: I can help you, if you like. I'm sure with your ability to think out of the box, we could come up with even better ways to structure the content of your next presentation.

When you use the six techniques for cultivating strong peer relationships, you'll find that you begin to embody the characteristics of good peer relationships – which are to act professionally, treat peers with respect, communicate clearly and often, be a trusted confidante, and encourage honest feedback.

Case Study: Question 1 of 3
Scenario

Analyze the characteristics of good peer relationships that Carrie and Luke display and the techniques they use to cultivate peer relationships.

Access the learning aid Carrie and Luke to help you answer the questions. Answer the questions in the given order.

Question

Consider the number of characteristics each person displays and the techniques they use to cultivate peer relationships.

Who is better at cultivating peer relationships?

Options:

1. Luke
2. Carrie

Answer

Option 1: This option is incorrect. Actually Carrie models the most characteristics of a good peer relationship and uses more of the techniques for cultivating a peer relationship.

Option 2: This is the correct option. Carrie models more characteristics of a good peer relationship and uses more of the techniques for cultivating the relationship.

Case Study: Question 2 of 3

Why is Carrie better at cultivating relationships?

Options:

1. Carrie communicates clearly and often, acts as a trusted confidante by listening well, encourages honest feedback, and treats others with respect
2. Carrie acts professionally at all times, encourages honest feedback, and treats others with respect
3. Carrie doesn't gossip, enjoys her work, helps others, and does what she says she'll do
4. Carrie, as a woman, has better emotional intelligence than Luke and so is better at building relationships

Answer

Option 1: This option is correct. Carrie is a good listener, is open to others' ideas, and lets people know how she's doing with her work when it affects them. She encourages honest feedback about the quality of her work. These behaviors illustrate that Carrie cultivates strong peer relationships.

Option 2: This option is incorrect. Although Carrie does encourage honest feedback about the quality of her work and treats others respectfully by being dependable and open to their ideas, she doesn't act professionally at all times. Sometimes she is silly and often confuses personal and professional relationships.

Option 3: This option is correct. Carrie doesn't join in when Luke gossips, she enjoys her work and shares her enthusiasm with him, and she often helps Luke when he has too much work.

Option 4: This option is incorrect. Gender is not a defining factor in emotional intelligence. Both sexes have strengths and weaknesses in building relationships with others.

Case Study: Question 3 of 3

Why is Luke not as effective at building peer relationships as Carrie?

Options:

1. Luke is not a trusted confidante and doesn't always treat colleagues with respect

2. Luke doesn't encourage honest feedback and doesn't communicate clearly and often

3. Luke gossips and often doesn't do what he says he's going to do

4. Luke doesn't provide positive feedback and doesn't help others

Answer

Option 1: This option is correct. Although Luke is helpful and provides positive feedback, he gossips and teases colleagues. This means he can't always be relied on to be a trusted confidante and he isn't always respectful.

Option 2: This option is incorrect. Luke does ask for honest feedback and always lets Carrie know if he can't deliver on his promises.

Option 3: This is a correct option. Luke has juicy stories about others, which may prevent Carrie from confiding in him. Although he is helpful and provides positive feedback, he often isn't able to provide the help he has offered. This reduces his trustworthiness and could distance him from Carrie.

Option 4: This is an incorrect option. Luke doesn't pretend Carrie's mistakes haven't happened, but provides her with encouragement and potential solutions. He does try to help others but often can't deliver.

CHAPTER 2 - Developing Strategic Peer Relationships in Your Organization

Section 1 - Being Aware of Your Working Environment

Becoming aware of the political environment in your workplace and using office politics appropriately can help you do your job better and achieve your work-related goals. Although all workplaces are political environments, they can be categorized as minimally, moderately, or highly politicized. Similarly, people differ in their approaches to office politics. They can be classified as purists, team players, or individualists.

Becoming environmentally aware

Becoming environmentally aware

To meet your goals at work, it's likely you have to interact with your colleagues and with people in other departments. Just working hard or putting in long hours isn't enough. The relationships you have with others also contribute to your success in the workplace.

Inter-functional relationships are those between people with different functions or expertise in an organization. For example, two people in different company departments may have an inter-functional relationship.

Efficient organizations rely on constructive and positive peer relationships between individuals across departments and functions.

Office politics inevitably affects inter-functional relationships. People instinctively protect their spheres of interest in order to advance their own interests or the interests of their teams or departments. In addition, people naturally take care of those they've created alliances with and strive to reciprocate favors.

Office politics is often perceived as being negative. For example, you may associate the term with dishonest, malicious, or just plain petty behavior in the workplace.

However, office politics is largely about forming productive, professional relationships – or beneficial alliances – with your peers.

Constructive interpersonal relationships at work can help you do your job better and achieve your work-related goals. To succeed in an office environment, you need to determine your own goals and cultivate the work relationships that will help you achieve these. You also have to be aware of the political climate in your workplace if you're to navigate it successfully.

Determine your goals

Once you've determined your goals, you can work toward achieving them. Just focusing on your work in isolation isn't enough. You also need to establish and cultivate the work relationships that will enable you to get the resources or support you need. It's worth considering this question – do your relationships at work currently support your goals or someone else's?

Navigate political environment

Every workplace is a political environment. You need to be aware of the political climate in your office if you're to build beneficial peer relationships. For example, what kind of office culture does your organization have and what type of employee is rewarded?

Not all organizations are the same or equally subject to office politics. They fall into one of three categories –

minimally politicized, moderately politicized, or highly politicized.

Minimally politicized

Minimally politicized workplaces are the least common. Largely undivided workforces characterize them. Cliques seldom form and employees focus on group achievements rather than the development of their personal reputation and power. A base level of respect exists among employees and subterfuge maneuvers rarely occur, although interpersonal favors and exchanges often take place.

Moderately politicized

Moderately politicized workplaces are typical of fast-paced, results-driven businesses, in which formal rules of conduct govern employee behavior.

Value is placed on interpersonal relationships and teamwork, so political maneuvering is mostly benign. When underhanded politicking occurs, it's usually very subtle, even if unspoken rules do exist. If conflict arises from politics, it can be difficult to detect the source of the problem and resolve it.

Highly politicized

Highly politicized workplaces are highly divided, with definite "in" and "out" groups. Effective communication with management depends on political alliances rather than expertise or ability.

In this type of environment, unspoken political rules trump formal rules of conduct, which are used largely to enforce the will of those who have political power. Frequent messy conflicts that are difficult to resolve and tend to get others involved characterize this type of workplace.

The Denver branch of a legal firm is a minimally politicized workplace. Employees are friendly and polite, and there are few divisions among them. They try to get along with one other and there are only occasional disagreements in the office.

Employees focus on working together to achieve team goals. Many of the employees volunteered to work over a weekend to prepare for an important case in return for some additional days of vacation. When the firm won the case, the whole office celebrated the victory together.

The Denver branch shares prestige clients around the workforce. This gives each employee the opportunity to work with at least one prestige client. Employees avoid being drawn into conflict or gossip about how accounts are assigned.

The firm's Atlanta branch is a moderately politicized workplace. Each year a bonus is paid to the members of each team that meets its performance target. Employees therefore focus on achieving their team's goals.

There is a lot of co-operation within teams and team members often provide support to each other. However, conflict occurs from time to time between the different teams in the office.

One star achiever lobbied the partners to transfer a new paralegal to her team, even though the paralegal had been hired for another team. This was to ensure that the team had the necessary skills to complete a major project assigned to it.

The firm's office in Chicago is highly politicized. This office is highly divided into many cliques that can be divided into definite "in" and "out" groups. Employees in the "out" groups are never assigned to high-profile clients or cases and are usually passed over for promotion.

Senior executives compete against each for corporate client assignments and power. This has resulted in bitter rivalries between many individuals. They are openly confrontational and engage in subterfuge to make life difficult for each other. Employees are often drawn into these disputes and are forced to choose sides.

Authority isn't based on seniority or expertise. Some executives exercise much authority through the political alliances they have built up. Most employees therefore ignore the formal rules in favor of unspoken political rules. Employees often ignore their manager's instructions and use their political connections to get their way.

Case Study: Question 1 of 1
Scenario

An advertising agency is represented in three cities – New York, London, and Rome. As a management consultant, you spend a week at each branch. Select each location to find out more about the branch and then answer the question.

New York

The New York office has the fastest pace of the three offices you visit. The atmosphere is busy but friendly.

Vague employee groups are centered around a few office achievers, but you also notice everyone in the office working well together. When a team wins a big account, everyone celebrates its achievement. You observe a junior designer putting in extra work for a manager he usually doesn't work for. This results in the designer getting to work on a prestigious account, although more senior designers are available.

London

At the London office, it's clear that certain cliques exercise more power than others and that authority isn't based on seniority or expertise.

You witness a mid-level copywriter delegating tasks to a manager. The copywriter says this is because she's too busy working on a more important project. You also witness an argument about which team lead should be granted a meeting with a potential new client. The argument ends up involving two managers and the office accountant, and becomes so loud that everyone in the office can hear it.

Rome

The Rome office has a relaxed atmosphere. Employees treat each other in a polite and friendly manner. Everyone seems to be part of one large team.

While you're there, you observe an assistant offering to do some extra administrative work for the art director in exchange for an afternoon off to attend an event at her child's school.

Question

Match each office to the appropriate political level.

Options:

A. New York
B. London
C. Rome

Targets:

1. Moderately politicized
2. Highly politicized
3. Minimally politicized

Answer

Peer Relationships

The New York office has the characteristics of a moderately politicized environment. Politicking is subtle and can work positively for the business. Value is placed on teamwork and results, and the pace of work is relatively fast.

London displays all the signs of a highly politicized office. Power is achieved through political alliances rather than through rank or expertise. There are definite "in" and "out" groups. Formal rules of conduct take second place to political maneuvering. Disputes are frequent and heated.

The Rome office can be classed as a minimally politicized environment. No clearly defined "in" and "out" groups exist – the mutual respect for everyone is evident. The work culture is easy going. Although employees may exchange favors, team work is highly valued and there are few angry interpersonal disputes.

Identifying political styles

Just like different offices, individuals differ in the extent to which they participate in office politics. You can categorize most people as purists, team players, or individualists.

Purists

Purists are the least political of all employees. They take the "straight ahead" approach and view hard work as the main method for achieving goals. Purists follow the rules. What they say is what they mean. In turn, they tend to be trusting and sometimes even naive. They're best suited to working in minimally politicized environments.

An example is an office clerk who puts in an honest day's work each day, refuses to be drawn into interpersonal work conflicts, and tells the truth even if it reflects negatively on him.

Team players

Team players abide by formal rules, but are willing to use political maneuvering to achieve team goals. They thrive in moderately political environments.

An example is a programmer who works hard and focuses on the achievements of her team, rather than specifically on her own achievements. She occasionally makes use of her friendly relationship with a senior manager to obtain additional resources for the team, but wouldn't consider asking for personal favors.

Individualists

Individualists are the most political. They follow or invoke formal rules only if this will result in personal advancement of some kind. They negotiate work relationships for personal gain, rather than viewing hard work or teamwork as the key to success. Whether openly aggressive or more underhanded, individualists are usually distrustful of the motives of others and flourish in highly politicized environments.

An example is a municipal officer who gives preferential use of public advertising space to agencies that can help sponsor her campaign for the position of mayor. Her clear goal is the advancement of her career. Her current job, along with its rules, takes second place.

Case Study: Question 1 of 1
Scenario

You've been working at an accounting company with a moderate to highly politicized culture for the past three months. In that time, you've had a chance to observe the working style and interpersonal relationships of three of your peers. Select each person to find out more and then answer the question.

Charles

Charles is a junior accountant who has just been promoted to team leader in his department. He's quiet and polite unless people get in the way of his goals. He reveals little about himself in his interpersonal encounters with others. He has built sound relationships with managers and others in power positions in the office. Over time, you notice that Charles is subtly using his relationships with managers to make life difficult for those he views as career path rivals.

Gillian

Gillian has been with the company for a number of years. Some of her friends fill management positions. She works hard and her peers like her. She calls for favors from allies only when she believes it will help her colleagues and department excel. She believes that a little bit of interdepartmental competition is healthy for business.

John

John is a junior accountant. He is friendly and polite, and follows office policies at all times. He makes a conscious effort to avoid being drawn into disputes or gossip. He has been passed over for a promotion once, despite the generally excellent quality of his work.

Question

Match each employee to the appropriate political style.

Options:

A. John
B. Gillian
C. Charles

Targets:

1. Purist
2. Team player

3. Individualist
Answer

John displays all the characteristics of a political purist. He shuns politics and underhanded methods of self-advancement in favor of hard work.

Gillian is a political team player who uses interpersonal politics only for the benefit of her team, rather than to advance her own career. She abides by office rules of conduct and rarely gets into disputes with other employees.

Charles is a good example of a subtle individualist. He uses his relationships with those in authority specifically for personal gain and is strictly focused on advancing his own career.

Not only should you be able to identify individual political styles, it is also important to match them to the appropriate political environment.

Purists thrive in minimally politicized environments. They are trusting and aren't motivated by prestige and power and they avoid getting involved in office politics. Even if they are highly capable, they usually get sidelined in a highly politicized workplace.

Team players flourish in moderately political environments. They focus on group relationships and performance and are willing to get involved in office politics to further the interests of the group they belong to.

Individualists are best suited to highly politicized workplaces. Unlike the purists, they enjoy office politics and work the system to derive power and prestige.

Case Study: Question 1 of 2
Scenario

Jennifer is a newly employed graphic designer in a design agency. She works closely with three people who were hired at the same time as her. They all work on the same team, reporting to a team leader and then to a manager. Each colleague has a distinct approach to navigating the sometimes precarious politics in this high-stress environment. Select each person to find out more and then answer the questions in any order.

William

William is an aggressive extrovert who doesn't shy away from arguments and always stands up for his own interests. He's careful to try and get people on his side, and goes out of his way to make friends who can assist him in his career path. He hopes eventually to lead the department.

Carly

Carly has a bubbly personality and seems incapable of thinking badly of anyone. She actively avoids conflict, as well as gossip. She's diligent and often works extra hours to make sure her work is of a high quality. During her first week, she ended up being given a lot of extra team administrative work simply by being accommodating, although she was already working overtime.

Britney

Britney is friendly and outgoing. She focuses on the achievements of her team and actively tries to persuade her manager to give the team a prestigious assignment so that it can prove itself. She avoids interpersonal conflicts unless there's no other way to defend her team's interests.

Jennifer

Jennifer has noticed that a core group of favorites seems to end up with the prize projects, while others are often overlooked. Design is a competitive industry, so some conflict is to be expected. However, Jennifer thinks the design agency's environment is constantly beset by petty power plays and squabbling for rank.

Question

Carly has a bubbly personality and seems incapable of thinking badly of anyone. She actively avoids conflict, as well as gossip. She's diligent and often works extra hours to make sure her work is of a high quality. During her first week, she ended up being given a lot of extra team administrative work simply by being accommodating, although she was already working overtime.

How would you describe the political environment of the design agency?

Options:

1. Minimally politicized
2. Moderately politicized
3. Highly politicized

Answer

Option 1: This is an incorrect option. In a minimally politicized office, employees aren't divided into political groups and disputes are rare.

Option 2: This option is incorrect. Although moderately politicized offices have some group divisions, the focus is usually on the broader team and these environments aren't characterized by frequent interpersonal disputes.

Option 3: This is the correct option. The office is plagued by political disputes, and employees are divided into distinct "in" and "out" groups. Power and rewards depend on alliances rather than formal position or expertise.

Case Study: Question 2 of 2

Match each colleague to the appropriate personal political style.

Options:

A. William
B. Carly
C. Britney

Targets:

1. Individualist
2. Purist
3. Team player

Answer

William is a good example of an aggressive and self-serving individualist. He thrives on conflict and focuses on using people to further his own goals.

Carly is a purist. She avoids office politics and instead focuses on hard work.

Britney is a team player. She uses office politics only to benefit her team, rather than for personal gain.

Section 2 - Identifying Key Peers
Section 2 - Identifying Key Peers

In a work environment, key peers are people who can help you achieve work-related objectives. It's important to determine who your key peers are. This will make it easier to achieve your work goals, get help when you need it, and identify suitable mentors.

To succeed, it's important to define your goals, identify your key peers, and then focus on building strong relationships with them. Key peers have special expertise, are suitable as mentors; have direct influence over your success; are able to provide support through assistance, advice, information, or protection; and are generally able and willing to help you achieve your objectives.

Importance of key peers

Importance of key peers

In an office environment, it's not just those senior to you who can affect your career. Instead of working in isolation, most people depend on information and various types of support from their colleagues and peers. Organizations depend on these links – or interdependencies – to be successful. The links are what convert groups of individuals into teams and separate departments into entities that can work together to achieve business goals.

If you don't have good relationships with your peers, you may not get the assistance or guidance you need to succeed in your work. You may be left out of the loop and so miss out on important information. It's less likely you'll be heard when you try to contribute to the ideas of a team. And when you face obstacles or crises like sudden deadlines, you may find that nobody is there to help you.

Having good relationships with your peers makes for a more comfortable and satisfying work environment. It can also help ensure that you achieve your work goals.

It's good to have strong relationships with all the people you work with. However, it's also true that some peers are more able to assist and support you than others.

Strategically, it's important to identify your key peers. These are the peers most able to help you accomplish personal and organizational goals at work.

You can then focus your efforts on building relationships with these people.

Focusing on building strategic relationships with key peers can have several benefits. It makes it more likely you'll achieve your work objectives, you'll find it easier to get help when you need it, and you'll be able to identify suitable mentors.

Achieve work objectives

If you have strong relations with your key peers, they can help you achieve work objectives and goals. They may help you improve your work, resolve problems, or speak in your defense.

For example, people with access to important information may provide you with information they know could be useful to you. Peers with special skills or knowledge may be willing to teach or guide you. Others may simply be willing to pitch in and help if you encounter problems or are struggling to meet a deadline.

Also, a peer may one day be promoted into a management position. If this person has reason to think of you as dependable and trustworthy, it's likely your career will benefit.

Easier to get help

Key peers include those who have the skills or knowledge to give you the help you need. If you have positive relationships with these people, it will be easier to ask for their help – and they'll be more willing to give it.

If you don't have strong relationships, people may give you only minimal assistance – for example, providing information only on a "need to know" basis. Or they may simply be unwilling to help at all, given their own busy schedules.

Say you develop a report for management, for the first time. If you ask a peer to review the report, this person is likely to provide you with comprehensive feedback. Someone else, who cares less what impression you make, might agree to review the report but may only check it briefly for any glaring factual errors.

Identify suitable mentors

Among your key peers are those who have skills and experience you could learn from. If they're willing to mentor or guide you, they can help you improve the quality of your work and develop your career potential.

It's ideal to learn from more than one key peer. If you have several mentors, you'll be exposed to different perspectives and may acquire a range of new skills, as well as enhance your existing skills.

Question

What are the benefits of identifying your key peers and establishing strong relationships with these people?

Options:

1. You're more likely to meet organizational goals, as well as your personal work goals

2. You'll find it easier to get assistance and guidance when you need it

3. You can improve your skills and learn new ones, which may develop your career

4. You'll avoid any conflict in the workplace

5. You won't have to work as hard to meet targets and will automatically be considered for promotions

Answer

Option 1: This option is correct. Key peers can give you the support and assistance you need to achieve work goals.

Option 2: This is a correct option. Key peers are those who can help you achieve your work goals. If you have strong relationships with them, it will be easier for you to ask for their assistance – and they'll be more ready to give it.

Option 3: This option is correct. Key peers include those who have the skills and experiences you can learn from. If they are willing to mentor you, your peers can help you develop your skills and advance your career.

Option 4: This is an incorrect option. Having good relationships with key peers can help shield you from the effects of unwarranted criticism or from attacks by rivals, but it won't completely prevent conflicts from arising. All workplaces are political environments, and some conflicts may be unavoidable.

Option 5: This option is incorrect. Having strong relationships with your peers can help you improve your performance and achieve your work goals. However, this doesn't mean you'll be given credit you haven't earned or won't have to work hard to advance in your career.

Identifying your key peers

Every workplace is a political environment, although some are more political than others. You should build relationships with all your peers but, to really succeed and thrive in your company's political environment, you can follow three steps. First determine your work goals, then identify your key peers, and finally build strong professional relationships with them.

1. Determine goals

It's only once you know in which direction you want to take your career that you can move forward. So if you want to succeed in your work and develop your career potential, you need to start by determining exactly what you want to achieve. For example, your goals could include expanding your skill set, reaching or exceeding a particular sales or productivity target, or moving into a more senior position.

2. Identify key peers

The nature of your goals will help determine who you identify as your key peers. For example, if your goal is to acquire specific skills, colleagues who have these skills and can help you acquire them are among your key peers. They can help you achieve your goal.

3. Build strong relationships

Once you've identified the key peers who can help you achieve your goals, you should focus your efforts on building strong professional relationships with them.

This involves developing your influence. It's about making things happen with and through other people, which is the cornerstone of a successful career.

You should identify certain characteristics in your colleagues when determining who your peers are:

- special expertise that can help you achieve your work objectives,
- suitability as mentors, together with the willingness to mentor you,
- influence over your success in reaching your goals,
- the ability to provide support through assistance, advice, information, and protection, and
- the ability and willingness to help in any way that assists you in achieving your objectives.

Peers with special expertise can help you learn new skills and improve your existing skills. So they can help you develop your career potential.

Say Jack works in a research team for an executive recruitment company. Andrea is the research manager. She works very efficiently and specializes in the recruitment of specialized technical talent. She can teach

Jack the skills that enable him to work more efficiently and provide him with relevant assistance. So in this case, Andrea is Jack's key peer.

People with specialist skills aren't necessarily your seniors. Members of a team may each have specialized skills in different areas, or even in different fields, and you may benefit from this. For example, Eve is a member of a marketing team who specializes in branding. Her colleague, Andrew, is a marketing strategist who knows all about the latest branding trends. Andrew is one of Eve's key peers. When she applies what she learns from Andrew, she'll release brands to the public in a more competitive way.

As well as specialist skills, you should search for peers who can serve as trusted counselors or teachers. Such mentors might include people who are slightly senior to you, or who have experience and knowledge you could benefit from.

Consider Oliver, who recently joined an international accounting firm as a junior accountant. Two of the people he identifies as key peers are Lori and Masaru. Both have experience and skills that could help Oliver achieve his long-term goal of moving into a senior management role.

Lori

Lori recently joined the company as a senior accountant. Lori has more experience than Oliver and a different perspective, particularly on international accounting methods, which she gained while working for a rival company. If Oliver develops a strong relationship with Lori, she can help him improve his work and teach him new approaches to the accountancy work he does.

Masaru

Peer Relationships

Masaru is Oliver's corporate controller. Masaru has many years' experience, special expertise, and an in-depth knowledge of the company. Oliver can learn a lot from Masaru, including how best to navigate the existing political environment in the company.

It can be difficult to get people with busy schedules, like Masaru, to spend time mentoring you – but it's more likely that they'll find the time to do this if you've already established a good relationship with them.

Among your key peers are those who have direct influence over you and your ability to achieve your goals.

For example, your team leader may have direct control over which work you're assigned and over your deadlines.

If you have a good relationship with your team leader, it's more likely you'll be assigned work that's considered important. It's also more likely that the team leader will be understanding and flexible if you're struggling to meet a deadline.

Peter has just started working for a sales team. Phillippa has been working as part of the sales team for over a year. Peter identifies Phillippa as a key peer because she can have influence over his success. If Peter has a good relationship with Phillippa, she's more likely to provide him with guidance and support, and to take an active interest in his development. She's also more likely to provide favorable reports on him to senior managers, who'll ultimately determine Peter's progress in the company.

It's not just people who have more experience or more political clout than you who make important allies. Anyone who supports you, providing day-to-day assistance, advice, information, or protection, is a key peer.

This often includes people you work closely with or interact with on a day-to-day basis. Colleagues who pass information to you, tell you how things work in the company, or are willing to help you meet a deadline can be invaluable.

For example, Troy recently started work as a member of a graphic design team at a magazine. He identifies Shirley, who's one of the other designers, as a key peer because she regularly checks that he knows what to do and has everything he needs to get the job done. She also reviews his work and picks up any mistakes, protecting him from the consequences of submitting work with errors to the team leader.

As another example, Steven starts work in a telephone sales team of 20 people. His manager expects him to start work without any guidance. Rose, who's sitting next to Steven, notices him struggling and offers help. She provides guidance and reassurance, and protects him by ensuring that the manager doesn't notice the difficulty he's having.

Essentially, any peer who has the ability to help you is a key peer with whom you should aim to build a strong relationship of mutual benefit. Help can come from anyone willing to provide it. Even someone who warns you when the manager is in a bad mood may be protecting you from a case of bad timing.

Sandra, an HR manager, identifies Raymond, the administration manager, as a key peer who can help her. Raymond is in constant communication with all the departmental heads and therefore knows their activities and whereabouts. If she has a strong relationship with Raymond, Sandra can ask him for information that makes it quick and easy to find the people she needs to contact.

- Libby is a pharmacy technician in a locally run pharmacy. She's studying at night via correspondence to become a pharmacist. She has several key peers:
- Violet is the nurse at the pharmacy who provides primary health care advice. Libby often talks to her about the side effects of medications that Violet administers. Violet's expertise helps Libby understand her course work on the typical side effects of the mediations better.
- Paula is the pharmacist who acts as Libby's mentor. She knows about Libby's aspirations and provides practical feedback to her that she can incorporate in her studies.
- Jason is another pharmacy technician. He is one of Libby's key peers because he has a lot of influence over Libby's success. He has been in the role for over a year and has the ability to provide day-to-day guidance, and provide positive feedback to management.
- Paula is also Libby's support base. When Libby has to take time off at short notice to write an exam or to complete an assignment, Libby knows that Paula will put in a good word for her to their manager.
- Rick used to be a pharmacy technician and now is a pharmacist. Like Libby, he took his degree via correspondence. Libby regards him as an ally because he's gone through the same hardships of

working and studying at the same time. She finds that he helps her with good practical coping strategies.

Question

You work as a sales representative in a company that markets a range of health products.

Who are your key peers?

Options:

1. Ashley, a member of the team who has specialized experience in marketing strategy that she's willing to share with you

2. Jacob, who works on the research team and can provide you with information about the products you're selling and how they work

3. Colin, a sales representative, who often updates you about developments in the company

4. Hazel, a friendly administrative assistant who always knows who you should call when things go wrong

5. Claire, who works in another department and with whom you have little or no day-to-day contact

6. Sam, a junior designer who you've helped mentor since he joined the company

Answer

Option 1: This is a correct option. Ashley would make an ideal mentor as she has special expertise you can benefit from. She also has the ability to provide guidance on a daily basis as you'll be working closely together on the same team.

Option 2: This option is correct. You will be more likely to succeed if you understand what you're selling. Therefore, Jacob is one of your key peers, as he can provide you with knowledge and understanding and has a direct influence over your success.

Option 3: This is a correct option. Anyone who supports you by keeping you updated or by providing assistance, advice, information, or protection, is a valuable ally and a key peer.

Option 4: This option is correct. Anyone who can assist you in some way and is willing to do so is a key peer. Hazel is an important ally because she can direct you to the right people when things go wrong.

Option 5: This is an incorrect option. Claire can't be a key peer if you don't have any contact with her. A key peer is someone with expertise, someone who has mentored you, someone who has influence over the work you do, someone who acts as your support base, or someone who helps you achieve your objective.

Option 6: This option is incorrect. You're more likely to be a key peer to Sam because you've helped mentor him.

Question

Joan has just started working as an accountant for a busy restaurant chain.

Who are Joan's key peers?

Options:
1. Luke Bishop – accountant
2. Carrie Flores – budget team member
3. Jeff Collins – junior marketer
4. Julia Harken – supplier accountant
5. Cody Hill – administration manager
6. Millie Logan – accountant

Answer

Option 1: This option is correct. Luke is a suitable mentor for Joan. He offers constant guidance and assistance, and protects her from making mistakes by checking over her work.

Option 2: This is a correct option. Carrie has direct influence over Joan's ability to achieve her goals, so it's important to develop a strong relationship with her.

Option 3: This option is incorrect. Jeff Collins has not much knowledge of accounting, and also doesn't have much experience as he's a junior. So Jeff isn't one of Joan's key peers.

Option 4: This is a correct option. Although Joan rarely sees Julia, on the few occasions when they do meet, Julia is willing to help. So in this case, Julia is one of Angela's key peers.

Option 5: This option is correct. Although Cody's job is unrelated to Joan's, he's willing to help Joan in any way he can and so is one of her key peers.

Option 6: This is an incorrect option. Millie isn't completing her own work to a high standard. Key peers should help you improve your work overall.

Section 3 - Building Strategic Relationships with Key Peers

Section 3 - Building Strategic Relationships with Key Peers

Establishing beneficial relationships with key peers can help ensure you achieve your work goals. Strategies for doing this include demonstrating emotional intelligence, establishing collaboration, helping peers achieve their goals, offering favors, and showing respect.

Once you've established strategic relationships with key peers, it's vital to maintain them. However, you should avoid becoming a doormat. You should distance yourself from those known as troublemakers in the office, and accept blame for your mistakes while sharing credit for successes.

Building peer relationships

Having beneficial professional relationships with your peers requires more than simply doing your jobs side by side in the same office. A level of trust and communication has to be established before you can make social trades with people who can help you achieve your goals. In terms of advancing in your career, building strategic relationships with key peers ranks alongside expertise and experience in importance.

A key requirement for building strategic peer relationships is that you exercise emotional intelligence when communicating. Take the example of Audrey and Betty, two employees at a busy advertising agency. Betty is heading a new advertising campaign and would like some input from Audrey, who works in the Design Department.

Follow along as Betty and Audrey discuss a favor required for an upcoming project.

Peer Relationships

Betty: Hi Audrey! If you have a moment, I'd like to run an idea past you. We recently spent a few days on location and I could use a fresh pair of eyes.

Audrey: Sure Betty, how can I help?

Betty: Can you take a look at these photos for the new campaign I'm working on – I'm going for an Art Deco feel with those sets.

Audrey: Let's take a look. Well, alright, I see what you're trying to do here, but those colors don't work. I'd probably get a different model too. This girl's just not right!

Betty: OK. This is the direction the client was going in, but what about it do you think doesn't work?

Audrey: The color scheme makes it look like a circus – I'd tone it down.

Betty: I see how that could improve it. What do you think of the layout?

Audrey: I'd take some of the drapes out. The layout would then have an authentic Art Deco look. Sorry if I'm stamping on your idea Betty, but you did ask me.

Betty: No problem at all. I value your input Audrey.

Through the conversation, it's clear that Betty is skilled at building strategic relationships. She remains polite and direct, despite the criticisms she receives from Audrey.

Instead of defending her own ideas, Betty invites Audrey's opinion to establish collaboration and listens with interest.

By demonstrating emotional intelligence, and being open to the input of others, Betty is able to turn what could be a negative encounter for some people into a beneficial and constructive one.

Emotional intelligence refers to your awareness of emotions – your own and those of others – and your ability to control your behavior in response to these. Emotional intelligence can help you build strong relationships with key peers. It enables you to develop and demonstrate a genuine interest in others so that an emotional connection is formed. For example, instead of instinctively defending her own work, Betty modifies her behavior in order to get more from her relationship with Audrey.

To develop emotional intelligence, you have to improve your awareness of emotions, which means you monitor your own feelings as well as those of others.

For example, if you're meeting with a particularly aggressive colleague, giving way to your natural "fight or flight" reaction may result in conflict. If you show weakness, you may end up being bullied.

Once you recognize your emotional triggers, you can learn to control your emotions so you aren't locked into learning negative behavior patterns. In other words, stepping back from your emotions gives you a chance to analyze the situation and react appropriately – instead of instinctively.

Demonstrating emotional intelligence in your work relationships can have several benefits. It equips you with the information and understanding you need to build a rapport with others, and so influence others to help you. And it generally results in a better work experience.

Influence others to help you

Emotionally intelligent people display a genuine interest in others and can modify their behavior based on context. They're sensitive to other people's feelings and generally have an understanding of the reasons why they behave in the ways they do. This helps them build rapport and establish mutually beneficial relationships. In these types of relationships, social trades take place more readily. People are driven to help one another – to give favors and reciprocate by returning those received.

If you don't demonstrate emotional intelligence, your attempts to establish relationships with key peers are likely to come across as insincere and manipulative.

Better work experience

Studies have shown that emotional intelligence results in a better work experience. Employees with higher emotional intelligence perform better than others who have similar skill levels, and get along better with other people. This translates into better job satisfaction and performance.

For example, managers at a large cosmetics manufacturer tracked the performance of two groups of salespeople. One group was hired for their skills and experience, the other for their high emotional intelligence levels. The result of the study showed that the second group achieved far greater sales results and were less likely to resign within the first year of employment.

It's important not to mistake emotional intelligence for simply getting along easily with people, and being generally happy or self-motivated. These are all positive traits, but have little to do with the ability to analyze and control emotions using emotional intelligence.

Question

Which are examples of ways that you can use emotional intelligence to help build strategic relationships with peers?

Options:
1. Recognizing the weakness in others and subtly exploiting it to your own advantage
2. Being aware of your own emotions and modifying potentially negative behavior
3. Showing an interest in others and earning their respect
4. Staying optimistic in the face of criticism and negative feedback on a project

Answer

Option 1: This is an incorrect option. Demonstrating emotional intelligence involves showing respect and interest in others, and building mutually beneficial relationships – rather than coldly manipulating others.

Option 2: This is a correct option. Being emotionally intelligent means being able to recognize your emotions and modify your behavior to get the most out of any situation.

Option 3: This option is correct. Emotional intelligence equips you to make real connections with people by showing genuine interest in them and earning their respect. In turn, this influences people to help you.

Option 4: This option is incorrect. Being positive does not mean the same as being emotional intelligent. People might be impressed by your positivity, but if you can't analyze their behavior and respond accordingly, you won't succeed in building strategic relationships.

Demonstrating emotional intelligence is key to building relationships. However, there are other steps you can take to develop and maintain these relationships. You can establish collaboration with key peers, help your peers with their goals, offer favors, and demonstrate mutual respect.

Establish collaboration

One way of connecting with a key peer and building rapport is through collaborating on a task or on solving a problem.

For example, you're a copywriter for a magazine. You've identified a team member who has excellent contacts as a key peer. You suggest that you and this person collaborate to create a particular feature article, in line with strengths you can contribute. In the process of working together, you can make it clear that you value the other person's opinions and work, and offer your input and help when it's required. If the article is a success, you can both share the credit – and your peer is likely to be far more ready to help you with your goals in the future.

Help your peers

If you help your peers achieve their goals, it's likely they'll be willing to help you in return.

Say you work for an interior design company and are always ready to help your team members – you review their ideas when asked, help to complete time-consuming assignments, and even give someone who missed the last bus home a lift. Members of your team will most likely be happy to help you in return when they can.

Offer favors

A good way to get people on your side is to offer favors when you have something of value to give. If you have specialized skills in a particular area, for example, it's likely your help will be welcomed. Then when you need something, the person you assisted in the past will want to return the favor.

Consider an IT manager with specialized programming knowledge. The manager offers his help to other departments, saving them time and money. In return, they're happy to oblige when the manager needs a favor done in his department.

Demonstrate mutual respect

Demonstrating respect for your peers is a basic requirement if you're to build mutually beneficial relationships. To show respect, you should practice active listening when talking to others – use physical cues to show you're paying attention, avoid interrupting the other person, ask questions to clarify issues when appropriate, and paraphrase to demonstrate your understanding. Also acknowledge that opinions contrary to your own are valid and generally behave in a manner that's polite and considerate.

Say you work at an adult education center. The staff contingency consists of a diverse group of people. Differences of opinion – and petty disputes – are common. Being known as the sensible person who shows respect to everyone will earn you many allies, who are likely to help you when necessary.

Case Study: Question 1 of 3
Scenario

Corbin works in the library of a university's law faculty. He's working his first shift with Emily, who recently transferred from a library on another campus. Since he's working closely with her, he intends to establish a beneficial peer relationship. During the course of the day, they talk about various subjects and Corbin tries to determine how he could collaborate with Emily, and help her achieve her goals or help her with a favor. Corbin receives an e-mail about creating a new section in the library, and he and Emily discuss how they'll accomplish this.

Answer the questions in order.

Question

Which librarian is more skilled at building strategic peer relationships?

Options:

1. Corbin
2. Emily

Answer

Option 1: This is the correct option. Corbin demonstrates empathy, listens carefully to Emily's complaint, and shows an interest in her hobby. He offers her help with her work in an attempt to establish collaboration and shows her a new way to catalog items. All these actions indicate that Corbin is skilled at building relationships.

Option 2: This option is incorrect. Emily shows interest only in herself and isn't able to empathize with Corbin, despite him using his free time to do her a favor.

Case Study: Question 2 of 3

Which examples of what Corbin does demonstrate he's emotionally intelligent?

Options:

1. Corbin states that the urgent work is simply part of the job
2. Corbin offers to help Emily with the task of setting up the catalog
3. Corbin is interested in Emily's pottery course
4. Corbin orders the tasks so that Emily's task must be completed first

Answer

Option 1: This option is incorrect. Corbin is just thinking out loud and hasn't adjusted his behavior to react to Emily's distress.

Option 2: This is a correct option. Corbin reacts to Emily's reluctance to do extra work with empathy and an offer to help, which is meant to ease her distress.

Option 3: This is a correct option. Instead of demanding that Emily do her share of the work, Corbin continues to put her at ease by taking an interest in her personal life.

Option 4: This option is incorrect. At this point, Corbin is unaware of Emily's stance on overtime, so he's just ordering the tasks in the way he thinks is the most efficient.

Case Study: Question 3 of 3

What could Emily have done to foster a mutually beneficial professional relationship with Corbin?

Options:

1. React calmly and listen to Corbin's plan and then stating her objection to overtime in a professional manner

2. Offer to miss an evening class to help with the urgent work

3. Tell Corbin she shouldn't be considered for overtime in the future

4. Leave the office at the normal hour because overtime isn't mentioned in her employment contract

Answer

Option 1: This is a correct option. Instead of immediately reacting with irritation, Emily could have modified her response so it wouldn't alienate Corbin.

Option 2: This option is correct. Emily could have modified her anger and been aware that her refusal to work would mean extra work for Corbin.

Option 3: This is an incorrect option. This doesn't take Corbin's emotions or work share into account.

Option 4: This option is incorrect. This would have been the flight response to the situation, which is just as alienating as the fight response she used on Corbin.

Maintaining peer relationships

Maintaining peer relationships

After taking the steps to get key peers on your side, you need to maintain the strategic relationships you've established. Every relationship needs work – it's a growing entity that responds to influence, not a product bought off the shelf. Relationships can fade if untended, or grow in counterproductive directions, with the result that you lose your allies and the respect you've worked hard to build.

Although it's good to help your key peers and offer them favors to establish relationships, it's possible to cross the line and be too consistently obliging.

You should be helpful, but you should avoid being taken advantage of. You don't want to become the person who agrees to do all the unpleasant tasks. Allowing this to happen will ultimately lose you the respect of your peers.

Say a junior bank clerk volunteers to help out a few senior team members and his manager with time-consuming administrative work in an attempt to gain their support and forge relationships. The clerk has

only the vague goal of career advancement in mind. He soon finds himself working huge amounts of overtime and struggling to complete his own work.

Unless a key peer really needs your support or help, or you hope to achieve a specific goal, making yourself the go-to-person for every problem or unwanted task will only give people the expectation that you can handle this at all times.

If you feel as though peers are taking advantage of you, it's vital to push back and put a stop to the situation.

If you find yourself in this position, you need to be as positive as possible. Avoid any disagreements that could alienate you from your peers. Also make sure you're entirely aware of all factors in the situation so you can deflect any challenges.

You can provide a good business reason why you can't accept specific work, give an example of a similar situation that didn't work, or call on a senior ally to state your case.

Provide a business reason

If you give a good business reason for people to stop taking advantage of you, it will be more compelling than a personal reason.

As an example, you could point out that although you'd be happy to complete a report on behalf of a manager, doing this would prevent you from attending to one of your core responsibilities, such as preparing a presentation for an important client. This makes it clear that you can't take on the extra work without this having negative business consequences.

Give an example

Giving an example of a similar situation that went badly is an effective way to make it clear that you shouldn't accept work that's not your core responsibility. This applies especially if there's risk involved.

If a colleague asks you to fill in for her by meeting her client, for example, you might politely point out that last time you met with someone else's client, it went very badly indeed because you weren't familiar with the client's history or preferences. This is a more diplomatic way to decline the request than just saying no.

Call on a senior ally

Sometimes enlisting the help of a senior ally is an appropriate way to prevent others from taking advantage of you.

If you have a friend in management, for example, that manager could make a friendly request to others to stop giving you work that isn't your core responsibility.

Other ways to maintain strong relationships with key peers are to distance yourself from the office "kicker" – or troublemaker – and to accept blame and share credit with peers whenever possible.

Distance yourself from the kicker

Distance yourself from the office kicker – an employee who is unpopular with management and others – because the association could cast you in a negative light.

If you form a close relationship with a colleague who constantly fights management and has a reputation for being difficult, some of that negative reputation is likely to rub off on you. This may lead others to be wary of forging or continuing a relationship with you.

Accept blame and share credit

Peer Relationships

You should accept blame for mistakes and share credit for achievements to maintain key peer relationships.

If you receive praise for a successful project, it's only right to pass that praise on to others that worked on it. This will endear you to those colleagues, who will likely reciprocate when possible. If you're criticized, however, be sure to accept the blame for what went wrong rather than attempting to shift the blame to others.

Question

Which examples illustrate the good ways in which you can maintain healthy relationships with key peers?

Options:

1. Avoid being a pushover and doing favors for no reward
2. Identify the "in" and "out" groups in the office, and ostracize anyone in the "out" group
3. Don't form a close association with the known office troublemaker
4. Take responsibility for your own mistakes, but acknowledge the role of others in every success
5. Make sure to be constant company for the most popular person in the office

Answer

Option 1: This option is correct. Avoid becoming a corporate doormat if you wish to maintain healthy and reciprocal peer relationships.

Option 2: This is an incorrect option. Actively alienating people will mark you out as petty and possibly damage your existing peer relationships.

Option 3: This option is correct. You must distance yourself from the office kicker, or you may gain a negative reputation by association.

Option 4: This is a correct option. Accept blame and share credit if you wish to endear yourself to others and be on the receiving end of reciprocal gestures.

Option 5: This option is incorrect. Trying too hard to get on the good side of one person will damage your relationships with other peers and may even annoy the person you're trying to impress.

REFERENCES

References
1. **Organizational Consulting: How to Be an Effective Internal Change Agent** - 2003, Alan Weiss, John Wiley & Sons
2. **Working Relationships** - 1999, Bob Wall, Davies-Black Publishing
3. **Breaking Through: The Making of Minority Executives in Corporate America** - 1999, David A. Thomas and John J. Gabarro, Harvard Business School Press
4. **Survive Office Politics: How to Steer A Course Through Minefields at Work** - 2004, , A & C Black
5. **The Communication Problem Solver: Simple Tools and Techniques for Busy Managers** - 2010, Nannette Rundle Carroll
6. **The 17 Essential Qualities of a Team Player: Becoming the kind of Person Every Team Wants** - 2002, John C. Maxwell, Thomas Nelson

7. **Working Relationships: Using Emotional Intelligence to Enhance Your Effectiveness with Others, Revised Edition** - 2008, Bob Wall, Davies-Black Publishing

www.ingramcontent.com/pod-product-compliance
Lightning Source LLC
Chambersburg PA
CBHW020927180526
45163CB00007B/2918